Preface

Every country has its own oral traditions of myth and legend, and the stories in this series come from the four corners of the earth. They will help the modern child to appreciate how happenings may be interpreted in different ways by people whose entire way of thinking may, for many reasons, be different.

The series is intended for an age range of 7 + to 11 + , with more easily understood stories in the first two books and more difficult concepts in the two later books.

Harry Stanton
Audrey Daly

Contents

WIDE RANGE

Myths and Legends

4

Harry Stanton
and Audrey Daly

Oliver & Boyd

Illustrated by Donald Harley, John Harrold,
Nicholas Hewetson, Annabel Large, Michael
Strand, Pat Tourret and Joanna Williams.

Oliver & Boyd
Robert Stevenson House
1–3 Baxter's Place
Leith Walk
Edinburgh EH1 3BB

A Division of Longman Group Ltd

First published 1983

ISBN 0 05 003363 8

Printed in Hong Kong by
Wing King Tong Co. Ltd

Mahon
McMahon

The Giant's Causeway in Northern Ireland is so strange and awe-inspiring to look at that many stories such as this one have grown up around it.

      *   *   *   *   *   *

On the day that Philip Rowan was born, he sneezed. This was taken to be a sign of great intelligence, and so it proved, for he learnt to read and write in no time at all, and he grew in knowledge and wisdom rapidly.

Then, when he was just seven years old, Philip disappeared. Search parties scoured the countryside, some on foot and some on horseback, but he could not be found. His parents, Maurice and Margaret Rowan, offered a large reward to anyone who could find the child, but no one claimed it. The boy had vanished without trace.

Several years passed, and nothing was heard of Philip Rowan. Then one night, something strange happened.

In a nearby village lived a blacksmith called Robin Kelly. He was a craftsman who could shoe a horse or forge a ploughshare better than anyone else.

On this particular night, he had gone to bed early, very tired, and he began to dream. He dreamed that he saw Philip Rowan, riding a magnificent white horse. The boy cried out to him that the giant Mahon

McMahon had carried him off. Philip was serving him as a page, deep in the heart of the giant's causeway.

"I have served the giant for seven years, and my period of service ends tomorrow night. Come and rescue me, and your fortune will be made."

"How do I know that this isn't just a foolish dream?" asked the blacksmith.

"If you want proof, you shall have it!" said the boy. And as he spoke, the white horse kicked out with its hind leg and caught the blacksmith upon the forehead.

Robin Kelly woke with a start, to find that his head was aching. He ran to the mirror and saw that there, upon his forehead, was the mark of a horseshoe. The dream was true!

The blacksmith sat and thought about the giant's causeway for a while. He had seen it many times— enormous stacks of rock like a colossal staircase, rising from the depths of the sea to form a huge cliff. People said that the giant Mahon McMahon lived deep in the heart of the cliff.

At last the blacksmith decided to go out to rescue Philip Rowan and seek his fortune, just as he had been told to in the dream.

Next day, as he left his smithy, he picked up a ploughshare with which to defend himself should he meet the giant. He walked all day until he came to his uncle's house, just across the bay from the giant's causeway.

When his old uncle heard about Robin's dream, he offered to row him across the bay, so as dusk was falling, they set out. It was a peaceful night, and the sea was calm. Before long, the boat was in the shadow of the great rocks. As they rowed along the cliff, Robin Kelly looked in vain for a cave opening that might be an entrance to the giant's palace.

He began to think he had been foolish to believe in his dream. Just then his uncle noticed a feeble light upon the face of the cliff. As they watched, the light grew slowly brighter, until they could see a doorway. The old man rowed the boat up to the cliff and Robin, his ploughshare in his hand, crept through the doorway into a passageway.

It was a strange place. The rocks on either side seemed to form themselves into fearful faces which changed as he walked by. The more the blacksmith looked at them, the more terrifying they became. Grasping his ploughshare tightly, Robin hurried along the passageway until he came to a huge room. The light of a single lamp showed him a gigantic figure, sitting at a massive stone table.

It was the giant Mahon McMahon! When he caught sight of Robin Kelly, the giant leapt to his feet in surprise.

"Who are you?" he shouted in a voice that rumbled like thunder. "What do you want?"

The blacksmith was terrified, but he was a brave

man. "I have come to claim Philip Rowan, whose period of service ends tonight," he answered.

"And who sent you here?" demanded the giant.

"No one sent me—I was told to come in a dream," said Robin Kelly.

"If you want him, you must pick him out from among all my other pages," said Mahon McMahon. "And if you make a mistake, you will die. Then the boy will remain with me for ever."

The giant led the blacksmith into a big room where there were hundreds of young children, all dressed alike in bright green tunics, and all about seven years old.

"Choose!" said the giant. "But remember, you have only one chance!"

The blacksmith did not know what to do, for there were so many young boys, and he could not remember what Philip Rowan looked like.

He walked round the room several times, but he could not see Philip Rowan, and the giant roared with laughter.

Then the giant said, "Let me see that little toy you have in your hand!" So the blacksmith gave him his ploughshare, and the giant twisted and turned it as if it were a piece of cloth, chuckling as he did so.

This made all the children burst out laughing, and as they laughed Robin Kelly heard someone call his name. He looked to one side and saw a boy staring at him. When the laughter died down, the blacksmith went over to him and took his hand. Then he said in a clear voice, "This boy is Philip Rowan."

"Yes! Yes! Yes!" shouted the other children, and as they shouted, the great room was plunged in darkness. The ground began to shake, and a sound like thunder echoed round the stony walls, but the blacksmith held fast to the boy's hand.

Then the ground seemed to heave, there was a blinding flash of light, and the blacksmith and the boy found themselves standing at the top of the giant's causeway, just as the sun was rising.

Mr and Mrs Rowan were overjoyed to see their son once again, and the blacksmith received his reward.

Strange to say, although Philip had been away for seven whole years, he did not seem one moment older than on the day he disappeared. In time, he too became a blacksmith, and lived to a ripe old age.

The Seal Woman

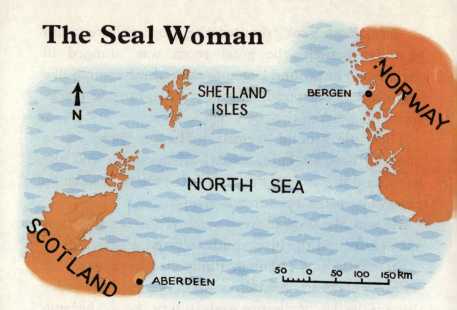

Although the Shetland Isles are now part of Scotland, they were once part of Norway; Bergen in Norway is the same distance away as Aberdeen in Scotland. The spirit of the Viking explorers is still alive in every Shetlander, and is part of their great heritage of legend.

*　　*　　*　　*　　*　　*

A rich Shetland farmer was walking one evening across his lands, which were close to the edge of the sea. There was a little sadness in his heart, for he was a lonely man. Once, long ago, he had been married to a tall, graceful woman, but she had died soon after their marriage. For the past fifteen years he had lived by himself, but he had prospered until now he was the biggest landowner on the island.

As he wandered along the cliff tops in the moonlight, he heard the sound of laughter and voices above the rippling of the waves, and he wondered who it could be. He looked down to see a group of young people dancing on the beach below. Their bodies swayed, and their arms moved like seaweed drifting in the tide.

They did not know that anyone was watching them, and the farmer kept very quiet and went on looking. Then he saw a pile of sealskins near them.

"The seal people!" exclaimed the farmer to himself. He had never before believed the story of how the seal people would come out of the sea and discard their skins, so that they could dance upon the beach like human beings.

He leaned forward to get a better view, and his foot slipped. A boulder bounced down the cliff face, and the dancers stopped. Snatching up their sealskins, they raced towards the sea.

One of the dancers was some way off down the beach, and before she could reach her skin, the farmer slithered down the cliff face and seized it. Tucking it under his arm, he climbed quickly up the steep path which led to his farm. Then he placed the sealskin in an old chest and buried it in the field behind his barn. Then he walked back to the beach.

He smiled to himself as he came to the edge of the cliff. If the stories of the seal people were true, he knew that one of them would not be able to return to the sea because he had her skin. He would be the first human to have seen a seal person close to.

Down the beach he saw a young woman with long black hair which reached to her waist. Her eyes were like dark pools, and her skin was as white as sea foam. Only her webbed fingers showed that she was from the sea.

"Please give me back my sealskin," she cried piteously. "Give it back to me, or I cannot return to the sea. Please let me have my skin back."

As he looked down at her, the farmer knew that he had never seen such a beautiful woman before. He wanted her for his wife. The seal woman pleaded with him until dawn lit the sky. When she saw that he would not return her sealskin, she walked with him to the farmhouse.

"If you won't let me go, then I must stay with you," she said. "But I fear that the future will only bring you unhappiness. One day I will have to return to my people."

The farmer and his bride from the sea were married in the village church. Everyone was pleased that their respected neighbour had a wife again, and wished them happiness.

As time passed, the couple had three sons, who all had thinly-webbed hands just like their mother's. The farmer loved his wife greatly, and he believed she loved him.

Then one night he awoke to find his wife quietly creeping out of bed. She slipped a cloak round her shoulders, and softly left the house.

He followed her, and in the starlight she walked to the cliffs overlooking the sea. She whistled softly, and a reply came from the sea. A great seal swam to the shore and went to her. The farmer could hear them talking in a language he could not understand, but he could feel the sadness in their voices.

He was very upset as he hurried back to the farmhouse to be in bed when his wife returned. He did not want her to realise that he knew her secret. He pretended to be asleep when she came back, and hoped that as time passed she would forget the people of the sea.

But she did not. Night after night she would wander down to the sea to talk with the seal people. Because she always returned, her husband ceased to worry about her nightly wanderings. Soon he learnt to sleep through her comings and goings, and so he did not hear her weeping when she returned.

The years went by, and their three sons grew into strapping young lads. Then one day when their father was away, they were playing in the field behind the barn, and saw a corner of an old chest sticking out of the ground.

One ran to fetch a spade, and soon the chest was out of the ground and open. There lay their mother's sealskin, which the farmer had hidden so many years ago.

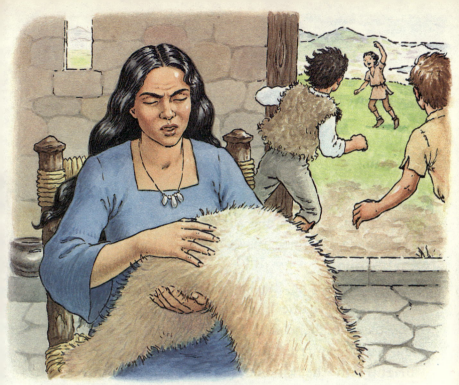

"Look what we've found!" they cried, taking the sealskin into the house to show their mother.

She trembled as she moved her hand over the soft sealskin. She knew that it was hers.

"It's lovely!" she exclaimed, and the boys scampered out of the house to the field in the hope of finding more buried treasure.

The seal woman sat quietly weeping. Now she had to choose—between the land and the sea. The happiness of being able to return to the sea gave her no pleasure, when she thought of leaving her sons behind. She would never see them again.

For many hours she sat, her heart torn in two by the choice she must make. By evening, she had made up her mind.

Not long after she kissed her children goodnight, her husband came home. In the yard, he found the chest in which he had hidden the sealskin. His heart sinking, he hurried into the house. A lantern burned brightly in the kitchen, but no one was there. He hurried upstairs to his children's bedroom. The boys were all safely asleep. From room to room he went, searching for his wife, but she was not there.

With a cry of anguish he rushed to the cliff top, just in time to see his wife transform herself back into a seal.

"Come back! Come back!" he cried. "Come back to your husband and your children."

From the sea a great seal swam towards the shore. It was the seal which had so faithfully visited her during all the time that she had been forced to live on land.

"Don't go, we need you too," cried the farmer.

The great seal waited at the water's edge while the seal woman turned towards the farmer on the cliff top.

In a soft voice, she spoke to him. "You have been a good husband, but you would not let me go. The sea has always called me back. I tried to love you, but I couldn't forget my first husband, who has faithfully visited me all through the many years that I have lived with you. He is waiting for me by the edge of the waves to take me back to our home beneath the sea." She paused, weeping.

"The sea is where I belong. Give my love to my sons, and when they are old enough, tell them why I had to leave them."

The seal woman dived into the sea and swam to the side of the great seal—her sea husband.

And as the farmer watched sadly, a lonely man once more, the two seals swam away.

Robin Hood and the Abbot of St Mary's

One of the greatest English folk heroes of all time was Robin Hood, an outlaw noted for robbing the rich to give to the poor. Though no one knows for certain just when he lived, it was probably at the end of the twelfth century. Sherwood Forest near Nottingham is the scene of most of the stories about him.

     *   *   *   *   *

The first frost of autumn was still upon the ground as Sir Peter of Papplewick rode through Sherwood Forest towards his home.

Although the sun was bright on the leaves, and birds sang cheerfully, Sir Peter was not a happy man. His head hung upon his chest and tears ran down his cheeks.

He saw nothing of the beauty of autumn. He did not even see the little group of outlaws blocking the road.

Without a word one of the outlaws grabbed the bridle, and Sir Peter's horse came to a standstill.

He was so sunk in gloom that for a moment Sir Peter was even unaware that his horse had stopped. Then he looked down at the outlaws, and realised who they were.

"All I have in my purse is one shilling!" he said quietly.

The outlaws looked at one another in disbelief.

"A knight with only one shilling in his pocket?" asked Much the Miller's son.

"That's all the money I have in the world, and the day after tomorrow I shall have nothing—not even a home to live in." He was so unhappy that he did not care what they thought. What did it matter?

"That can't be true," said Will Scarlet. "I know who you are. I've seen you before and I've even been in your castle. You are Sir Peter of Papplewick, and you own the lands to the north of the river Leen."

"Only for one more day," said the old knight sadly. "Then, as happened to your master, Robin of Locksley, my home and lands are to be taken from me."

"In that case, come and meet him," said Will Scarlet, and they took Sir Peter through the forest to a camp hidden in a fold of the hills.

There, sitting beneath an oak tree, was Robin Hood, fixing a new string to his bow.

He saw them approach, and stood up to greet Sir Peter as he dismounted from his horse.

"It's good to see you again, Sir Peter," he said warmly.

For a while they sat beneath the oak tree and talked of times long gone, when men were free from tyranny.

That was before King Richard went off to the Crusades, leaving his country and his people to suffer at the hands of greedy barons and churchmen.

At last Robin Hood asked Sir Peter, "Why do you look so sad?"

"Because tomorrow the Abbot of St Mary's is going to steal my home and my lands that have belonged to me and my family for over two hundred years."

"How can he do that?" asked the outlaw.

"When I came back from crusading in the Holy Land last year, I found that my son was in prison, wrongfully accused of treason. To get him out, I had to borrow money, to pay the lawyers' and the judges' fees. I borrowed that money from the Abbot of St Mary's—and if I can't repay it by noon tomorrow, he will claim the lands for himself."

"Have you asked him to give you a little more time?" asked Robin Hood.

"I asked him this morning," replied Sir Peter. He paused, thinking back. "The greedy monk wants my lands, to add to all the other land he has stolen. There's no hope at all." The old knight's head drooped as he finished speaking.

"I should have left the Abbot of St Mary's in the duck pond when I threw him into it," muttered Friar Tuck, who had been listening.

"Cheer up, Sir Peter. All is not lost," said Robin Hood. "You will keep your castle, I promise you.

Friar Tuck will bring you the money before noon tomorrow."

"Shall I?" queried Friar Tuck.

"Oh yes," replied Robin with a twinkle in his eye. "I have a plan."

One of the biggest outlaws—Little John—took Sir Peter back to the road, and stayed with him until they were in sight of the old knight's castle, before bidding him farewell.

"Where do you think we are going to get the money from?" asked Friar Tuck, as the outlaws talked together later.

"From the Abbot himself! If he is going to collect money from Sir Peter, then he will also be collecting money from Nottingham. The Abbot's treasury will certainly be following that wicked old monk!" laughed Robin Hood.

From early in the morning next day, the outlaws waited beside the Nottingham road. Not a leaf moved nor a twig snapped, although over a hundred men lay hidden in the greenwood.

As the sun rose higher into the sky, the distant sound of a galloping horse could be heard.

It was their lookout. He had been waiting just outside the gates of Nottingham, ready to report to Robin Hood as soon as the Abbot appeared.

"The Abbot is riding this way with an escort of soldiers. His treasury and many guards are not far behind him," he announced.

"It's the treasury we want," said Robin. "We will let the Abbot go in peace."

Half an hour later the Abbot rode past, followed by the soldiers.

"There is no sign of the terrible Robin Hood," sneered the Abbot as he passed close to the outlaws.

Robin Hood was near enough to have sent an arrow through the Abbot's black heart, but he sat back with a quiet smile on his face.

A quarter of an hour later, the Abbot's treasurer appeared, guarded by fifty soldiers.

He rode slowly, for the pack horses carrying the Abbot's treasure were heavily laden.

A sharp blast on Robin's hunting horn was the signal.

Immediately a hundred outlaws appeared on both sides of the road, each man with his bow drawn and a deadly arrow at the ready.

The treasurer and his guards were surrounded and outnumbered, with no time to draw their swords.

"We will take your pack horses," announced Robin Hood, coming forward.

"One day you will hang!" scowled the treasurer.

Without fuss three outlaws cut the pack horses loose and led them off. There was silence and no one moved for the space of five minutes, until the pack horses had disappeared into the forest.

Then, as silently as they had appeared, the outlaws slipped away.

"After them," shouted the treasurer. One guard began to follow the outlaws into the greenwood, but an arrow thudded into his shoulder and he stopped.

With a snarl the treasurer urged his horse forward, and galloped away down the road, followed by the guards.

A mile from the road, Robin Hood opened the packs on one of the horses. He counted out the exact amount Sir Peter owed to the Abbot, put it into a leather bag and gave it to Friar Tuck.

"Away to Sir Peter's castle, you old rascal, and pay the Abbot with his own money!" laughed Robin.

The fat monk rode swiftly through the forest on paths known only to the outlaws, and arrived soon after the Abbot.

A meal had been prepared at the castle, and the greedy Abbot was looking about him as he ate.

"At noon this will all be mine," he sniggered.

"Won't you give me more time?" pleaded Sir Peter.

"No! You have had a year, and now I must have the lands and the castle if you cannot pay."

Sir Peter was fast losing all hope, for there was no sign of Friar Tuck and the money Robin had promised.

Then the Abbot rose to his feet. "It is noon," he stated. "The castle is mine."

"Not so," said a gruff voice, and Friar Tuck appeared from the shadows. With a deep bow he gave the Abbot the leather bag.

The Abbot gasped as he recognised the fat monk. "You!" he bellowed.

"Me!" agreed Friar Tuck.

Some of the Abbot's men grinned, for they too recognised the fat Friar. When he had been a monk at St Mary's Abbey, he had thrown the Abbot into the duck pond. They had enjoyed that!

The Abbot's face grew red with anger. He tipped the gold coins into a large bowl, and slowly counted them.

Then he glowered at Sir Peter. "Unfortunately you have found the money in time," he snapped.

Then he turned and marched out, and never knew that the money he had received—was his own!

A Visitor to Sherwood

Three men dressed as monks rode slowly along the dusty road through Sherwood Forest. Although the day was hot, all three wore the hoods of their habits pulled well over their faces, as if they did not want to be recognised.

As they rounded a bend, a young man dressed in Lincoln green stepped into the road and raised his hand.

"Stop, my lord Abbot!" he said.

"And who are you?" asked the monk who wore an Abbot's chain.

"I am Robin Hood, and these are my men," said the outlaw, pointing to the bushes at each side of the road.

From the bushes stepped twenty men, all dressed in Lincoln green, each armed with a bow and a quiver full of arrows.

"I have no gold in my saddle bags," said the Abbot.

"What have you then, my lord Abbot?" asked Robin Hood.

"If you are indeed Robin Hood, then I have a message for you from the king," replied the man dressed as an Abbot.

"Any messenger from the king is welcome in Sherwood," said Robin. He signed to three outlaws, who took the bridles of the horses.

"Come, follow me," said Robin, leading the way through the greenwood.

For some time they went on, following little known paths, until they reached an open glade beside some tall cliffs.

At the top of the cliffs sat a lookout, and at their foot was a large cave, its entrance hidden by tall bushes.

"Welcome to our house!" said Robin Hood. "Spend today with us and tomorrow—after you have delivered your message—we will see you safely on your way."

The three strangers dismounted from their horses and looked around them.

In front of the cave the cooks were preparing the evening meal. Across a log fire, one of the king's deer was slowly roasting, turning on a spit. The delicious smell of the meat drifted across the open glade.

"Hungry, my lord Abbot?" asked Robin Hood, smiling.

"After a long day's ride from Nottingham, it's a pleasure to smell such fine cooking," said the Abbot, "but surely the king would be angry to know that you are hunting and eating his deer?"

Robin Hood shook his head. "No. We are loyal subjects of the king. We are only outlaws because the king is away fighting in the Crusades. While he has been away, there has been no justice in the land, and honest men have been driven from their homes and hunted like wild animals."

"Tell me what has been happening, for I too have been out of the country for a long time," said the Abbot.

Robin sat down on a log beside him, and talked until the sun sank low over the trees.

He told of how he had been driven from his own home, and how the poor people had to pay more and more taxes, while the rich people seemed to grow richer every day.

"The people of England are only slaves since the king went away to fight in the Holy Land," said Robin Hood angrily.

"Slaves?" asked the Abbot, looking puzzled.

"The barons call them serfs. They work all day for their masters, then have to give up half of the crops from their own land. And the friends of Prince John steal land from men like me who are loyal Saxons."

The Abbot spoke very little, although sometimes he asked questions. When Robin Hood and his men answered his questions, he seemed to grow angry.

Then, after a while, it was time to eat.

The outlaws had many trades, and not all of them were farmers and foresters. Some had been cooks and chefs in great castles.

So it was that, sitting in the middle of Sherwood Forest, the stranger wearing abbot's robes enjoyed one of the most delicious meals he had ever eaten. Leaning over the rough table, he helped himself to fresh salmon from the River Trent, venison from the forest together with freshly gathered mushrooms, wild fowl, vegetables from the countryside, and tiny wild strawberries.

As the meal drew to a close, the Abbot sat back. "I do declare, that was the finest meal I have eaten for many a day," he gasped, rubbing his stomach. "I have eaten too much, it was so good."

"I'm glad you enjoyed your meal. It is better than any of the villagers ever get," remarked Little John. He sat with his bow across his back, ready for action.

"Can you use that bow?" asked the Abbot.

The outlaws roared with laughter. "Here in Sherwood Forest, you'll find the best bowmen in the land!" exclaimed Robin Hood.

"Show me then!" said the Abbot.

Quickly the remains of the meal were cleared away. Down the centre of the glade Will Scarlet placed the targets—thin hazel wands. Tied to the top of each was a small posy of wild flowers.

With his first arrow, Much the Miller's son shot the flowers from the first target. His second split the hazel wand in two.

"Enough!" said Robin Hood. "Little John, let's see what you can do to the second target."

All eyes were on Little John. Slowly he bent the bow, leaned back and set his arrow racing through the evening air to graze the hazel wand and set it quivering. While it still quivered, a second arrow cut the stick in two.

"Well done! Well done!" shouted the Abbot.

Friar Tuck, a half-eaten chicken leg in his hand, bustled out.

"Let me try," he said, taking Little John's bow.

He sent three arrows one after the other into the next target, grunted with satisfaction and gave back the bow. Then he went on eating the chicken leg.

"Now it's your turn," said the Abbot, turning to Robin Hood.

The outlaw nodded, and called for his bow and arrows. A hush settled over the forest as he strung his bow. Then he pointed to a leather wine bottle hanging on a far tree, and carefully took aim. Three times in quick succession he bent his bow, sending three arrows into the air so swiftly that the third was on its way before the first had reached its target.

A great cheer rose up as one after another the arrows thudded into the bottle.

Then the onlookers grew silent again as Robin raised his bow to send his last arrow through the evening air—and sliced neatly through the thin rope

holding up the wine bottle.

"Never have I seen such marksmanship!" marvelled the Abbot. "It is true that the finest archers in England live in Sherwood Forest!"

Robin Hood smiled. Then he said, "Now that the entertainment is over, my lord Abbot, let us hear the message that you have from our good King Richard."

The band of outlaws gathered round them, and stood silent, looking at the tall figure of the Abbot.

"I have talked with you and I know that you are all loyal subjects of the king," said the Abbot. "I have also seen that the finest archers are all followers of Robin Hood, but you are nevertheless all outlaws and hunted by the soldiers of the barons."

The Abbot climbed on to a tree stump where all could see and hear him. "Before I came to the forest I heard many stories about you." He looked down at the outlaws, and paused for a moment. "Now tell me, would you all return home if the king were to pardon you?"

The men murmured, nodding their heads.

"Only the king could do that," said Robin a little sadly. "And he is far away in the Holy Land, fighting the Crusades."

"No, he is not!" exclaimed the Abbot, and as he spoke he untied the cord around his long black habit. As his cloak fell open, they saw rich red velvet and gold silk. This was no Abbot—it was the king of England!

There was an awed silence, then all the outlaws knelt before their king.

"You have my pardon," said the king. "You are all free men."

A moment passed, then a great cheer went up, making the very leaves quiver. It went on and on, until that great king, Richard the Lionheart, raised his hand for silence. He went to where Robin Hood still knelt and said gently, "Come, Robin of Locksley, you too are a free man. Your outlaw days are over!"

And long into the night the forest rang to the shouts and happiness of free men. Watching over them, King Richard and Robin Hood nodded to each other.

"A happy night," said the king.

"Amen to that," replied Robin.

The Story of Balder

The Vikings—or Norsemen—of Scandinavia were sailing the world from end to end long before King Alfred in the ninth century created the first British navy. They knew China, and it is even thought that they may have discovered America hundreds of years before Columbus landed in the West Indies.

They were fighting men of great courage, so it is not surprising that their gods—who lived in a far place called Asgard, ruled by Odin the all-seeing—were often warriors as well.

Norse legends are known as far afield as the men who invented them, for they took them to many lands.

★   ★   ★   ★   ★   ★

Odin the all wise, the most powerful of all the Norse gods at their home of Asgard, had many sons. Thor was the strongest; Balder was the best loved, for he was wise and merciful; yet another brother was blind and was always sad—his name was Hondur.

Everyone loved Balder, for he was always happy, and he taught men how to use herbs for healing wounds and curing illness.

Then came a time when Balder ceased to smile, and his face was always sad too.

"Tell me," said Odin, "why are you so unhappy?"

Balder paused for a moment before replying. Then he said, "When I sleep at night, I have nightmares. I dream that I am to die, but when I wake up I cannot remember how or when my death will come. All I know is that there is some danger."

All the gods were greatly worried at this news, so they sat talking long into the night.

At dawn Odin arose and saddled his eight-legged horse Sleipnir. He rode for nine days and nine nights until he came to the gates of the underworld. There he stopped and chanted a magic spell.

Slowly the ground opened, and out of it came the grey-green shape of a witch.

"What do you want?" she wailed.

"Tell me about Balder," he commanded.

"Balder the beautiful, the wise, will soon come to the underworld. A seat has already been prepared for him," she replied, without moving her lips.

"Old witch, tell me who will kill Balder!" said Odin.

"Hondur, his brother, will be the cause of his death," croaked the old crone. Then as Odin watched, she slowly changed into a wisp of smoke and was gone.

Odin stood for a moment in silence, thinking about her words. Then he climbed back on to his horse and rode home. As he went he thought of the many things he could do to save his son.

When he arrived back at Asgard, there was no unhappiness. Queen Frigga, his wife, ran to meet him.

"Balder is safe! I have saved him," she cried.

"How can this be?" asked Odin.

"There is no longer any danger. Everything in the world loves Balder, and all things have sworn not to harm him. Fire and water, iron and stone, birds and beasts, men, disease and poisons have all promised not to harm our son," said his queen. This news made Odin much happier.

Soon the gods discovered a new game. Nothing could touch Balder. He would stand laughing while they threw stones or shot arrows at him. Swords left no mark on him, and axes fell harmlessly to one side. He always remained unhurt. It was as if Balder wore invisible armour.

Then one day, Loki the evil one saw them. He watched for a while and was filled with jealousy. He hated the happy Balder, whom everyone else loved. So he changed himself into an old woman and hobbled to where Queen Frigga was sitting.

"Why are the gods throwing stones and weapons at Balder?" asked Loki in a rasping voice.

"It is because they know that nothing can hurt him. Everything has sworn me an oath not to harm my son. No sword or stone or anything that grows or moves upon the earth will harm Balder," replied Frigga.

"And have all the trees and plants and flowers agreed not to harm him?" asked Loki.

"All dangerous things have promised," replied the queen. "Indeed, only one thing has not taken the oath, but that's so small and weak that it wasn't necessary."

"And what was that?" asked Loki cunningly.

"Only the mistletoe which grows on the oak tree. It has no root, and it is soft and without strength."

After a while Loki hobbled off. As soon as he was out of Frigga's sight he changed himself back to his own form and went in search of the mistletoe.

Not far away he found a great oak tree with a bunch of mistletoe growing on it.

Loki broke off a piece which he shaped into a dart, then muttering an evil spell he breathed upon it and it became as hard as iron.

Then he went back to where the gods were playing. Only Hondur was not taking part in the fun.

"Why don't *you* throw something at Balder?" asked Loki.

"Because I can't see where he is, and in any case I have nothing to throw," answered Hondur.

"Let me help you," said Loki. "Here is a little twig of mistletoe. I will guide your hand."

He put the dart of mistletoe into Hondur's hand, then helped him to direct the throw.

The little twig flew through the air. It hit Balder and he fell dead.

There was a stunned silence and the gods were struck dumb with sorrow. Loki slipped away before anybody could stop him.

Poor blind Hondur stood quiet, not knowing that he had killed the brother he loved. When at last they told him, he turned and stumbled away into the forest, caring nothing if he lived or died.

The other gods still stood quietly, deeply troubled.

Queen Frigga stood back and looked at them all. "Who is going to ride down into the underworld to bring back my son?" she demanded.

The dead reached the underworld quickly and easily, but for others the journey was long and dangerous. The gods looked at one another, then—"I will!" shouted Hermod, the messenger of the gods. "I will ride to the underworld and ask Hela to let Balder go."

Without another word, he mounted Odin's eight-legged horse Sleipnir and galloped away.

*   *   *   *   *   *

As the sound of galloping grew faint, the gods carried the body of Balder down to the seashore. They placed it in his longboat, and the ship was pushed out on to the waves.

His wife Nanna was there. As she bent down to kiss him for the last time, her heart broke and she died. The gods placed her at Balder's side.

Thor took a lighted torch and set fire to the longboat as it left the shore.

For many hours the gods stood on the beach, tears streaming down their faces. At last darkness fell, and the flames lit up the night sky as the ship drifted out to sea. Then suddenly it was gone.

Meanwhile, Hermod was on his way to the underworld. He rode swiftly for nine days and nine nights until he came to a river of fire crossed by a narrow bridge.

"Who are you and what do you want?" asked the guardian of the bridge.

"I have ridden from Asgard to ask for the return of Balder. Is he here yet?" answered Hermod.

"Balder and his wife passed over the bridge nine days ago when they died," replied the guardian. "They are in Hela's palace."

Hermod crossed the bridge and rode on until he came to the gates of the underworld, guarded by a great dog which barred his way.

Hermod stopped and tightened the girth on his saddle. Then he jumped over the gates and the dog which guarded them, into the underworld. He rode on until he came to the great halls of Hela. There he saw Balder sitting with his wife Nanna, but he rode on until he found Hela, the queen of the underworld.

Fear clutched at Hermod's heart when he saw her, so terrible did she look.

"How dare you come here!" she screamed.

"I have come to beg for the return of Balder," said Hermod bravely.

"Why?"

"Because all the world weeps for him," replied Hermod.

"Then if all the world weeps for him he may return, but I will not release him until *everything* weeps for him."

She stood up and pointed to the door. "Go!" she commanded.

Quickly he remounted Sleipnir and rode back to Asgard.

When they heard the news the gods sent messengers throughout all the world asking everything to weep for Balder. The giants and the trolls wept for him, even the trees and the stones wept, but Balder did not return.

"I cannot understand why Balder does not come back," commented Hermod. "Although Hela is queen of the underworld, she would not break her promise. Perhaps someone or something is not weeping for him."

He went to see Odin the all seeing, all wise one. "Why has Balder not returned?" Hermod asked him. "I have travelled the world and all things weep for him. Even the giants, the dwarfs and the trolls weep for his return."

Odin listened to him, then his two ravens, which flew over the whole world and brought him news from far and wide, settled on his shoulders. In their hoarse cackling voices, they told Odin of all they saw.

When they had finished, Odin turned to Hermod and said, "Go to the cold far north. There in the mountains, you will find a cave in which a giantess lives who does not weep."

With a cry of anger, Hermod strode out of the castle and rode rapidly northwards. Far into the mountains he went, through dark narrow valleys strewn with rocks. Then he came to the snow fields, where his horse floundered through deep snow drifts. At last he found the home of the giantess who did not weep.

"Who are you, and why do you not weep for Balder?" asked Hermod.

"I am Thok. I weep for no man, for no man has ever wept for me," answered the giantess.

So Hermod told her about Balder and Hela's promise to release him if the whole world wept.

But the giantess only laughed harshly. "I will only weep dry tears for him. Living or dead, I care nothing for this son of Odin. Let Hela keep what she has."

Time and time again Hermod begged Thok the giantess to change her mind, but it was in vain. So in the end he rode sorrowfully away, with her cruel laughter ringing in his ears.

When he returned to Asgard, the gods listened in silent sadness to the news which Hermod had to tell.

"Then Balder must remain where he is," said Odin unhappily. At that moment, the two ravens settled upon his shoulders and whispered into his ears, and a great gust of anger took Odin. He rose to his full height, shaking with a terrible temper.

"I am told that Thok the giantess was none other than Loki in disguise," he thundered.

That night all the gods assembled in the great hall. None of them smiled, and a great sorrow hung over the gathering.

As they all sat eating, Loki came to the gates of Asgard. At the door he asked the guard, "Tell me, what are the gods talking about?"

"They are talking about you and the evil you have brought upon the world," replied the guard. "No one speaks any good of you."

"Then I shall go and eat with them, for they cannot harm me within the walls of Asgard," Loki said scornfully.

When Loki appeared, silence fell upon all the other gods. They sat looking with contempt and hatred upon their evil visitor.

"Give me food and drink, for I am hungry and thirsty after my journey," he commanded as he sat at the table.

No one moved to help him, so he grabbed a cup and took a long drink before rudely helping himself to food. With his mouth full, he leaned back in his chair and shouted, "Greetings to you all! Why are you all so miserable—won't Thok weep for Balder?"

"Hold your tongue!" ordered Odin.

"Only a coward like you would talk like that," sneered Loki.

"Be quiet," said Frigga gently.

"The witch speaks!" taunted Loki.

Thor rose up from his seat with thunder on his face. "One more word and my hammer will stop *you* speaking for ever," he roared.

For a moment or two Loki was quiet, but gradually he started once more to taunt the gods. He reminded Sif that he had cut off her golden hair, and that he had stolen the golden apples of Iduna. He sneered at all the gods one after the other, until Thor again rose to his feet. Then Loki knew that it was time to leave, and he slipped away to find a safe hiding place.

All the gods were now roused to great anger, and together they agreed not to rest until Loki was captured. They began to scour the world in search of him.

Loki hid at the top of a mountain where he built a house with four doors, one on each side, so that he could escape in any direction.

But he could not hide for ever from Odin the all seeing. One day when Loki looked from his house, he saw some of the gods climbing the mountain towards his house.

With a cry of anger, Loki slipped out of the back door. Turning himself into a salmon, he leapt into a river and hid in a deep pool beneath a waterfall.

Thor and the gods arrived at the house to find that Loki was not there.

"He must be hiding," roared Thor. "Odin said he was here in this house beside the waterfall."

"Perhaps he is hiding in the water," suggested Hermod.

"Then we shall need a net," decided Thor.

The gods set to work and, using some twine they found in the house, they made a long net.

Thor held one end of the net and the other gods took the other end and together they pulled it along the river bed. Loki swam ahead of the net, then he leapt over it and swam away.

Starting from further down the river, the net was dragged upstream by the gods, while Thor waded behind it in the middle of the stream.

Seeing that he was trapped, Loki tried to escape by leaping over the top of the net, but Thor reached out and caught hold of him by the tail. He held him so tightly that salmon have narrow tails even to this day.

Now that Loki was captured, he returned to his own shape. The gods showed him no mercy, for he had shown none to Balder. They took him to a cave far beneath the earth and there they bound him with iron bands upon three sharp slabs of stone. They left him there, guarded by a poisonous serpent.

There he struggled so much that the earth itself shuddered and shook, causing earthquakes.

And there he will remain until the end of the world.

El Cid

In the last half of the eleventh century, El Cid championed Christianity against the Moors, who were Moslems. He is a Spanish national hero, and his brave deeds are remembered throughout Spain in story and song.

*　　*　　*　　*　　*　　*

At one time, almost a thousand years ago, Spain was a land of constant wars. All the best parts of the country —the rich green valleys of the south, the fine fishing coast and the grass-covered plains—were in the hands of the Moors. The Moors were a fierce and warlike people, who had crossed the narrow Straits of

Gibraltar from North Africa many years before. They were feared by all. Mounted on their swift Arabian horses, armed with lances and curving scimitars, they shouted as they rode into battle, "Allah is God, and Mohammed is his prophet."

They had crushed the Christian kingdoms of Spain and had seized most of the country. Then they settled down to enjoy their conquests. They built fine palaces and cities. They did more, for with their knowledge of irrigation, they turned deserts into rich farmlands.

The Spaniards had been driven into the bleak mountains. Their lands were only desert plains and valleys with rocky soil. Defeat had made the Spaniards into a race of hardy warriors and their great ambition was to reconquer their land and drive the hated Moors from Spain back into Africa. The task was long and hard, and many thought it would be impossible.

The most powerful of all the Christian kings of Spain in those days was Fernando, King of Castile. In his youth he had been a mighty warrior; but in his old age he fought no more and was loved by his people and respected by his enemies. One day when the king was seated with his advisers he said,

"Now that I am old, we must decide who is to inherit the kingdom when I die. Should it go to my eldest son, or should it be divided into three kingdoms, one for each of my sons? Heralds must be sent to every part of the kingdom to order all our faithful nobles to attend a great council of state to decide the future of our kingdom."

Far and wide across the land the king's heralds sped with news of the great council. To the sound of trumpets, the royal command was made known throughout the kingdom, and all the king's nobles set off to attend the great council at court.

One herald went to give the news to Don Diego de Vivar, a very learned and wise man who lived with his family near the city of Vivar. On many occasions he had been called to advise the king about affairs of state, but his greatest pleasure was studying the history of Spain, and teaching it to his sons.

The royal herald found Don Diego seated in his library surrounded by books and maps and manuscripts. The old scholar listened politely to the herald's

announcement, then sighed. "You may tell his majesty that I have heard, and will obey, his command," he said.

When the herald had left, Don Diego muttered to himself crossly, "Really, I prefer the company of my manuscripts to the company of kings."

At that moment Rodrigo, Don Diego's eldest son, burst into the room. His eyes sparkled as he said, "Father, was that the king's herald? Is there to be a war?"

"No, it isn't war," replied Don Diego. "There is to be a great council of state, and I must attend."

"Father, may I go with you?" asked his son eagerly.

"No! You have not been invited. You are not a knight, and I cannot think that his majesty will need the advice of a seventeen-year-old boy!"

"But the journey to the court is a long one, Father," argued his son. "You might meet bandits or Moors on the way, and I could protect you!"

Don Diego laughed. "It's true that I'm an old man, but I'm too poor to be robbed by bandits. And there are no fierce Moors between here and the royal court."

"If I don't meet the king, I will never be knighted, because he won't know who I am," Rodrigo pointed out.

Don Diego sat thinking for a few moments. He did not want to disappoint his son. He said at last, "You are too young to be knighted, but I will take you to the great council so that you may see the royal court."

Rodrigo was very excited. His mother made him a new cloak of crimson velvet, and Rodrigo himself polished the high-backed saddle and the reins of his father's horse until they gleamed. The night before they left, he could not sleep.

When they set off next day, Rodrigo's mother, his two brothers, and their three old servants came to see them off. Although the family was noble, they were not rich, and they had only one horse. After kissing his mother farewell, Rodrigo mounted behind Don Diego to begin the long journey to the royal capital.

Evening came, and they stopped at a small inn by the side of the road. While Don Diego made arrangements for a room, Rodrigo took the horse to a nearby well. There he found several soldiers talking together as their horses drank their fill.

Suddenly there was a terrified cry. "Is there no Christian who will help me?"

Rodrigo and the soldiers rushed to help. It was a leper, sinking into a patch of quicksand, which was already up to his waist.

"For the love of God," he cried, "give me a hand to help me out."

When the soldiers saw the white patches of the terrible disease of leprosy on the man's face and arms, they drew back in horror, fearing that they too might catch it. But Rodrigo took pity on the man. Leaning over the quicksand, and steadied by the branch of a

tree, he stretched out his arm. He gripped the leper's hand and slowly pulled him from the quicksand.

Then he saw that the man was shivering, for he was almost naked. Rodrigo took off his new cloak, wrapped it round the leper's shoulders, and said, "They won't let you stay at the inn, but you may sleep in the stables next to my horse if you wish. The straw is warm and I will bring you some food."

The leper bowed his head in thanks, unable to speak. Rodrigo saw him safely to the stable, then returned to the well to get his horse.

The soldiers were still there, and they drew away from him. "You may already be infected!" they cried.

Rodrigo shrugged, unworried. "Only what God wills may come to pass," he answered.

He gave his horse some water, then took the animal

into the stable. The leper was sleeping on the red velvet cape, huddled in the straw. As Rodrigo groomed his horse, he decided that he would have to bring food secretly to the poor man. If Don Diego knew, he would be very worried.

A few hours later, after they had eaten and while his father snored loudly on the bed next to him, Rodrigo rose, took some food that he had saved from his own meal, and made his way to the stable. It was now past midnight.

He found that the leper had disappeared, and the red velvet cape was neatly folded beside the horse. Rodrigo was just about to return to the inn when he heard a voice behind him. "Are you looking for me, Rodrigo?"

Rodrigo turned. There, standing in the stable entrance, was a man dressed in a white tunic. A soft glow of light seemed to shine round him, though there was no moon that night.

"Who are you?" Rodrigo asked, in a trembling voice.

"I am Saint Lazarus, and you saved me from the quicksand. I am going to reward you. From now on, nothing and no one will defeat you. Your fame shall increase, for great victories will be yours."

Saint Lazarus smiled, raised his hand and then vanished. Rodrigo returned to his room, but that night he did not sleep.

The next day, as Rodrigo and his father rode through a rocky valley, their horse suddenly reared and stopped. Rodrigo jumped down and ran to some nearby rocks in case a band of robbers was waiting to attack them. Don Diego called after his son, but Rodrigo took no notice. He climbed carefully over the rocks and peered down. Then he stood up and laughed. There were no robbers, only a wild starving horse.

It was a stallion, thin and dirty and without a saddle. When Rodrigo approached, the horse allowed him to pat its neck. It was not really a wild horse, but one which had been abandoned by its owner.

Don Diego rode up. "What a sorry-looking beast!" he exclaimed. "It has been alone for a long time."

"In that case it shall be mine!" Rodrigo cried.

"You would have to be a *babieca* to want so forlorn

a horse," laughed Don Diego. By babieca, he meant a fool.

"So be it. I shall call him Babieca, and one day he will be famous," said Rodrigo, running his hands through the horse's tangled white mane.

"Well, it will certainly give my old horse a rest," admitted Don Diego. "Take the horse if you wish, but I fear that the world will laugh at you."

Rodrigo spoke softly to the stallion, then climbed on its back. "See, Father, he is going to let me ride him!" he said, pleased.

"Of course—he simply hasn't the strength to run away. You will make a fine sight riding into the royal court on a horse like that!"

"By the time we arrive at the capital, my Babieca will look just as good as your horse," Rodrigo replied.

That night he spent hours combing and grooming Babieca, and each day for the rest of the journey he gave the horse all that it could eat. He even managed to buy an old saddle from a soldier at one of the inns, and he polished it until it sparkled. By the time they arrived at the royal court, Babieca was a proud and beautiful horse.

★　　★　　★　　★　　★　　★

Rodrigo went with his father to the great Hall of Justice in the royal palace. Banners and pennants

hung on the walls, and rows of soldiers lined the walls with their lances raised. Every noble and knight in the kingdom was there.

The trumpets sounded, and Rodrigo found himself standing with his father close to the king. A herald stepped forward, and from a great roll of parchment called out all the names of those present. As each name was called out, a noble came forward to kneel before the king and offer him his sword. The king would then speak a few words and return the sword. Then the next name on the list would be called.

When his father's name was called, Rodrigo knelt with his father before the king. The old man presented his sword, and the king gripped it firmly and handed it back.

"May I present to your majesty my eldest son, Rodrigo?" said Don Diego.

The king's eyes turned to Rodrigo. "A fine young man, Don Diego! He looks like a soldier. Do you want to be a warrior?" he asked Rodrigo.

"Yes, your majesty!" Rodrigo exclaimed. "I would like to be a knight."

The king smiled. "You must first prove yourself before you can become a knight."

That afternoon Don Diego and some of the king's closest advisers gathered together to talk. Rodrigo spent his time in the stables, grooming their horses. Much later in the day, when Rodrigo was sitting on a bench outside the stables' entrance, his father appeared. Rodrigo had never seen him so angry.

"Father, what has happened?" he asked.

"I have been publicly insulted before the king," said the old man furiously. "After we had been talking for a long while, his majesty appointed me tutor to his three sons, which is a great honour. But the Count of Lozano, who had hoped to be the royal tutor himself, stood up and shouted that since I am not a warrior, I could only instruct the princes in cowardice! Then he slapped me twice across the face! If only I were a few years younger . . ." Don Diego fell silent.

Rodrigo's face grew red with anger. He stood up and said, "Father, you did not teach *me* cowardice. Give me your sword."

Don Diego smiled. "You speak as I hoped you would." He unbuckled his sword and handed it to Rodrigo. "This sword is named Tizone. In my youth it avenged many wrongs, Rodrigo. Let it do so now!"

Rodrigo took the sword, kissed his father on each cheek, and hurried to saddle Babieca. He mounted, and without a backward glance spurred his horse to a gallop.

It did not take him long to reach the castle where the count was staying. As he rode into the courtyard, he saw the Count of Lozano about to dismount from his horse.

"And what do *you* want?" the count demanded.

"Do not dismount. I am Rodrigo de Vivar. I have come to take back the honour that you stole from my father."

The count laughed rudely. "Go away, young man! You are not even a knight, and I am one of the best swordsmen in Spain. Go while you may!"

"It would seem that you only wish to fight old and defenceless men!" cried Rodrigo.

On hearing these words, the Count of Lozano grew purple with rage. He drew his sword, spurred his horse and charged against Rodrigo.

But his sword jarred against the sword Tizone, and Rodrigo pulled Babieca round quickly.

Then before the count had time to recover, Rodrigo was upon him, filled with rage. Tizone struck sparks of fire from the count's sword again and again, while Babieca reared, wheeled and charged like a true war horse. Standing up in Babieca's stirrups, his eyes ablaze, and waving Tizone on high, Rodrigo looked like a young avenging angel. Soon the count received such a blow that his sword clattered to the floor. Then Tizone smashed down through his armour. The count fell from his horse, mortally wounded.

Just as he fell, five royal heralds galloped into the castle courtyard. When they saw what had happened, they rode over to Rodrigo.

"We were sent by his majesty to try to prevent this," said one of the heralds. "Rodrigo de Vivar, you must appear before the king."

Rodrigo was brought before the king in the great Hall of Justice. Only the king and Don Diego were

there, looking solemn.

The king spoke. "Rodrigo de Vivar, you have proved yourself in the test of battle. Kneel before me."

Rodrigo knelt down, and with his sword the king touched him lightly on each shoulder. "In the name of God I make you a knight," he said.

Then he went on, "In killing the Count of Lozano you have committed a crime. The punishment for such a crime is banishment!"

Rodrigo stood up and bowed as the king finished speaking.

Later, with his father's blessing and the sword Tizone buckled at his side, he hurried from the royal palace.

Although Rodrigo left the court of King Fernando, he did not immediately leave the kingdom. Instead, he returned to Vivar, to bid farewell to his mother. News both of his victory and of his banishment had gone before him, so that when he reached his family home, several of his boyhood friends were waiting there, to go with him into exile. When at last he left his home town, he had a loyal band of followers.

From that time forward, hardly a day passed that did not bring news of the heroic feats of Rodrigo de Vivar. Everyone spoke of his bravery.

One day, as Rodrigo and his followers were riding along, they saw a rich caravan of heavily laden mules guarded by Moorish soldiers. Rodrigo led his companions in a charge, and soon the Moorish guards were fleeing for their lives.

Then Rodrigo and his men turned their horses to see what they had captured. Several Moorish merchants were still with the mules, and they threw themselves down in front of Rodrigo's horse.

"We know who you are, Rodrigo de Vivar, and we beg that you will not steal the treasure that we take to the Emir," said one of them.

When Rodrigo and his companions heard this, they smiled. "What is this treasure, old man?" demanded Rodrigo.

The merchant scrambled to his feet and walked over to the nearest mule, which carried what looked like a small tent on its back.

"See for yourself, Rodrigo de Vivar!" said the old merchant, drawing back the silk curtains.

Sitting inside was a young Moorish princess. Her lips trembled, and tears ran down her cheeks.

"This is the bride of the Emir. She is to be married within the week." And the old merchant let the silk curtains fall back into place.

Rodrigo sat silent upon his horse for a moment or two, then he spoke. "We must let them go," he declared. "We would not want to spoil a wedding. Go on your way, merchant, and give my best wishes to the Emir."

The merchant, his face wreathed in smiles, called down the blessings of Allah on Rodrigo and his men. Then, even as he was speaking, his lips faltered and he pointed with trembling fingers towards a cloud of dust on the horizon. A large band of horsemen was riding towards them.

When the horsemen came to within a hundred metres they halted and one of them, a gigantic man with a red beard, spurred his horse forward.

Rodrigo advanced to meet him. "Who are you?" he demanded.

The huge stranger grinned. "I am Gonzalvo—known as the Red Bandit!"

A wail went up from the Moorish merchants, for they recognised the name of the most feared bandit in all of Spain.

"Shall we put these Moorish dogs to death and divide their treasure between us?" he asked jovially.

"No. I have given my word that this caravan will not be touched," said Rodrigo quietly.

"Then we must fight, and as my men outnumber yours by three to one you will lose! You would have done better to share with us!" sneered Gonzalvo.

Rodrigo knew that there was just one chance—a fight between the leader of the bandits and himself, alone. He glanced behind him and saw that his men had drawn their swords, but he knew that they faced defeat. So riding up close to Gonzalvo, he suddenly reached out and plucked a hair from the bandit's heavy red beard.

He raised the hair on high and shouted to Gonzalvo's

followers, "See the hair that I have plucked from the beard of your cowardly leader!"

Now plucking a hair from a man's beard was the greatest insult that could be offered in those days. The bandit's face turned crimson with fury. Without another word he hit Rodrigo so hard that his sword Tizone went spinning out of his hand and into the dust.

Rodrigo faced certain death. Knowing that it would be but a matter of seconds before the gigantic bandit killed him, he wheeled Babieca behind Gonzalvo and sprang from his saddle, dragging the bandit to the ground.

They rolled and struggled desperately, and suddenly the bandit's sword went flying through the air to land next to Rodrigo's sword Tizone. In that same moment, Gonzalvo was on his feet. A dagger glinted in his hand, and he sprang at Rodrigo. Rodrigo rolled to escape the blow, jumped to his feet and raced to recover his sword. He snatched it up and turned to face his enemy.

"Very well, Rodrigo de Vivar," Gonzalvo gasped. "You have a sword, and I have none. You may kill me."

Without a word Rodrigo kicked Gonzalvo's sword back to him.

Now the two enemies circled each other. Suddenly Rodrigo thrust at Gonzalvo's chest. Gonzalvo gave a shout of triumph, sidestepped Rodrigo's thrust, and swung his sword towards his enemy's side—but his blade met nothing but air as Rodrigo himself sidestepped and brought Tizone whistling through the air to deal his enemy a mortal blow.

A great cheer rose from Rodrigo's followers when they saw Gonzalvo fall. The bandits, their leader dead, turned tail and fled as if pursued by demons.

Now the Moorish merchants clustered round Rodrigo, helping him back on to Babieca and praising him for his courage and swordsmanship.

They called him "El Mio Cid, Campeador," which meant, "My lord, the champion." And from then until the day he died, Rodrigo de Vivar was known throughout Spain by both Moors and Spaniards as El Cid.

The Story of Perseus

One of the greatest civilisations the world has ever known flourished in Greece nearly two and a half thousand years ago. The ancient Greeks were a vigorous, intelligent people; their ideas on many subjects—philosophy, medicine, architecture, athletics, for example—still form part of our civilisations today.

They had many stories of heroes who were more than life-size, with powers granted by the gods who lived on Mount Olympus and were ruled by Zeus, father of the gods.

*   *   *   *   *   *

Acrisius, King of Argos, was not a happy man. Although he had a beautiful daughter, he had no sons.

"Who will be the next King of Argos, if I have no son?" he wondered.

Time passed, but he had no more children. All he had was his daughter Danae, who had grown up into a lovely woman.

One day the king went to seek the wise man in the temple. "Tell me, wise man," he said, "tell me about the future."

For a long time the wise man sat thinking, speaking not a word, a far away look in his eyes. Then—"You

will live for many years yet," he said, "but you won't have any more children. Your grandson will be the next king—after he has killed you."

Then the wise man closed his eyes and said no more.

King Acrisius went back to his palace and thought about the wise man's words, then he became angry. If his grandson was going to kill him, there was only one way to stop it happening. He would make sure there was no grandson!

"Danae shall not marry anyone!" he said.

The next day he ordered his men to build a stone tower with a great brass door. His daughter was going to be locked away for ever, so that she could not be married or have a son.

All this time Zeus, the father of the gods, had been watching from his home on Mount Olympus. He saw the lovely Danae weeping in the stone tower, and he was sorry for her.

So it came to pass that one night, as she gazed unhappily from her tower, Danae had a visitor. Zeus himself had come to see her! She was so beautiful that Zeus fell in love with her, and without the knowledge of the king they were secretly married.

At the end of that year Danae had a baby, a little boy. She called him Perseus.

King Acrisius was beside himself with anger when he heard that Perseus had been born.

"I must get rid of them," he shouted. But he did not wish to kill his daughter and her son himself. He thought about it for a long time, then he said, "I know how to get rid of them!"

So he put Danae and her baby son into a large wooden box and nailed down the lid. Then two of his men carried the box down to the seashore and set it adrift. The king watched as it floated away. "Now if they die, it will be the gods' fault," he said in satisfaction.

But Zeus watched over the box. One day his son Perseus would be a great hero, and Zeus would not let him die. For a long time the box drifted across the sea until Dictys, a fisherman on the island of Seriphos, found it tangled in his nets.

Although Dictys was only a fisherman, he was the

brother of Polydectes, the King of Seriphos. Polydectes allowed Danae and her son to stay on the island, and for many years they lived with Dictys and his wife.

As time went on, Perseus grew into a strong, handsome young man. He could run faster, and throw the javelin and discus further, than anybody on the island of Seriphos.

Danae was still a very beautiful woman, and King Polydectes wanted to marry her. Danae refused, for she knew that he was a cruel man. In any case, the great god Zeus was her husband, and she did not want to marry any man.

Polydectes did not know why she would not marry him, but he thought it was because of Perseus. So he started to think of ways in which he could rid himself of the young man.

At last Polydectes thought of a plan. He pretended that he was going to marry a princess from a nearby island, and ordered all the young men to his palace to see what wedding presents they were going to give him.

As Polydectes knew very well, Perseus had no money; he was very poor. There was nothing he could give as a wedding present.

The king spoke to each young man in turn, then came to Perseus, who had no present for him.

"What, no gift? Have you no wedding present?" cried the king.

"Oh! Oh! Oh!" laughed the king's friends.

Perseus was angry. He thought that the king had asked him there only so that he could sneer at him.

"Well, if you can't afford to give me a present, go and get me the head of the Gorgon, Medusa. If you are brave enough to do so!"

Perseus was too angry to think clearly. "I will get it for you!" he said furiously.

The king smiled grimly, for Perseus had fallen into his trap. Now he would get rid of him, for nobody could get the Gorgon's head. None of those who had tried had ever come back.

King Polydectes knew all about the Gorgons.

They were three sisters, ugly monsters who had faces like women, but with tusks for teeth and snakes for hair. They had bronze wings and claws of brass. Medusa, the ugliest sister, could turn a man into stone with just one look into his eyes. This was what Polydectes hoped would happen to Perseus.

Perseus saw that there was no escape, and he walked out of the palace to start his search for the Gorgon's head.

And once again Zeus was looking after his son. Suddenly there were two people standing beside Perseus. One was a tall slim woman dressed in white, who wore a helmet on her head, and the other was a young man with wings on his hat and on his boots.

"Perseus, I am Athena, the goddess of wisdom

and this is Hermes, messenger of the gods. Zeus has sent us to help you," said the woman.

First she gave Perseus a shield which shone in the sun.

"Take this shield," she said. "It is brightly polished like a mirror. Look at the Gorgon Medusa in it, and then you will be safe. If you look straight at her and she looks into your eyes, you will be turned to stone."

Then it was Hermes' turn. "Take this sickle; it will never break and it will cut through anything at a single stroke." He handed Perseus a hat, a bag and a pair of winged sandals, and said, "This is the hat of darkness. When you wear it you will be invisible. With these sandals, you will be able to fly. And when you cut off Medusa's head, put it into this bag."

"One last word—go to the Grey Sisters, for only they can tell you where the Gorgons live," said Athena.

Then, as suddenly as they had appeared, Hermes and Athena were gone.

With the magic sandals on his feet, Perseus flew north over the mountains to a land of cold mists. There, on a beach, sat the three Grey Sisters. They were so old that they had only one eye and one tooth between them, and these they shared. They were the only people in the world who knew where the Gorgons lived.

Perseus put on his hat of darkness and crept up silently behind the Grey Sisters. Just as they were

passing the eye and the tooth to one another, he
snatched them away.

"Where's the tooth?" squeaked one of the sisters.

"I don't know. I can't see, where is the eye?"
muttered the second sister.

"Give me the tooth, give it to me," moaned the
third sister. "I want to eat. How can I eat without
the tooth? I like eating."

"Who has got the eye? Who has got the eye?"
cried the first sister.

"I have the eye and the tooth," said Perseus.

"Give it back! Give it back!" squeaked the sisters.

"Not until you tell me where the Gorgons can
be found," replied Perseus.

"No! No! Never! It's a secret," they said together.

"Wicked boy! Give back the tooth. I want to eat,"
screamed the third sister.

"Tell me where to find the Gorgons and you can have your tooth and your eye back," Perseus told them.

For a while the three sisters muttered to one another, until at last one of them said, "North, young man, north. Go north to the Island of Storms."

After they had told him how to get to the Island of Storms, Perseus gave them back the eye and the tooth. Then he flew northwards through rain and snow.

Perseus stopped and rested a while until it was night before he finished his journey to the Island of Storms. He was hoping that the Gorgons would be asleep.

Hovering over the island, without looking down, Perseus put on his hat of darkness. Then he turned Athena's shield so that he could see the Gorgons in its bright surface, lit by the moonlight. They were asleep, surrounded by men and animals they had turned to stone.

Keeping his eyes fixed on the shield, Perseus flew down. With one swift blow he cut off the head of Medusa, and pushed it quickly into his bag. Then he sped away on his winged sandals.

The other two sisters sprang after him with terrible screams, their wicked brass claws flashing in the moonlight. They were so close behind that he could hear the snakes on their heads hissing, and he flew faster and faster until he could hear them no more.

He flew southwards until he reached the north coast of Africa, where he found Atlas the Giant holding up the sky on his shoulders.

With a voice like thunder, he asked Perseus where he had been and where he was going.

When he heard that Perseus had Medusa's head, he begged that he might see it.

"Please let me look at it. I am old, and tired of holding earth and heaven apart. I want to turn to stone," said Atlas.

So Perseus held up the Gorgon's head for a moment, and slowly the giant became Mount Atlas. His white hair changed into snow, his clothes into forests of tall trees. No longer would Atlas have to hold up the sky.

As Perseus flew towards home he saw a young woman chained to the rocks beside the sea. She was crying, and he could tell that she was very frightened. Her name was Andromeda.

"Why are you here?" asked Perseus.

"My mother boasted that she and I were more beautiful than the sea nymphs, and Poseidon the god of the sea has sent a horrible sea serpent to punish us for our pride. It will only go away if I am sacrificed."

"I will save you," said Perseus, but before he could cut the chains that bound her to the rocks, they heard a great roar. Andromeda screamed, and Perseus turned to see the sea serpent racing across the waves.

Great clouds of spray rose as the monster lashed the water into white foam.

Perseus flew high above the serpent, then darting down from the sky he buried his sickle in the

monster's neck. Time after time he slashed, but he could not kill it. He could only wound it. So at last he pulled the Gorgon's head from his bag and held it for the monster to see. The monster turned to stone and sank beneath the waves.

Then Perseus cut the chains that bound Andromeda to the rocks, and took her back to her father.

"What can I give you?" asked the king.

There was only one thing Perseus wanted! He had fallen in love with the beautiful Andromeda and she had fallen in love with him. "I wish to marry your daughter," he said.

The king was happy to hear the hero ask for his daughter's hand in marriage. He gladly gave his consent and the next day the people cheered at the wedding of Andromeda and Perseus.

Only one man was not happy—Andromeda's uncle. Many years before, when she was only a tiny girl, Andromeda had been promised to him in marriage, but when she was in danger, he had done nothing to try to save her.

Just as the wedding was taking place, the doors burst open and there was her uncle with some armed men.

Perseus had no sword, so he pulled the Gorgon's head from its bag.

A second later the flashing swords of his enemies were still as the men were turned to stone.

Not long after the wedding, Perseus and Andromeda set sail for the island of Seriphos, in one of her father's ships. When they arrived, Perseus discovered that his mother had been locked up in a temple because she would not marry Polydectes. She was dying from hunger, for the king would not allow any food to be taken into the temple.

Cold with anger, Perseus rescued his mother from the temple and left her with Andromeda, while he went to see King Polydectes.

"Oh, look who has come back!" jeered the king as Perseus entered the palace. "Has our brave young man brought back the head of the Gorgon Medusa?" The men round him laughed at his words.

Perseus waited silently for the laughter to stop.

"Well, have you got the Gorgon's head?" sneered the king again.

"Yes," replied Perseus.

"Then suppose you let us see it!" said Polydectes, grinning.

"Are you sure you *want* to see it?" asked Perseus, warningly.

"Of course," said the king, laughing. "Show us."

"You will never sneer or jeer at me again, then!" said Perseus. He took the Gorgon's head from the bag and held it up before Polydectes and his court, and instantly they all turned to stone.

As Perseus left the court, Athena and Hermes

appeared before him once more, and he gave them back the gifts they had lent to him. To Athena, he gave the Gorgon's head.

Now that Polydectes was dead, Dictys became king and he ruled much more wisely than his brother had done.

Time passed, and Perseus decided to go back to Argos, where he had been born.

His grandfather, King Acrisius, heard that Perseus was on his way, and became worried. He remembered what the wise man had told him. Secretly he left the city, and went to see his friend the King of Lorissa. He was surprised to find that Perseus too was at Lorissa, taking part in the games.

Perseus threw the discus, and as usual was much better than anyone else. With his last powerful throw, the discus soared into the air and a sudden gust of wind blew it to one side. It hit King Acrisius, killing him instantly.

So in this way the words of the wise man in the temple came true at last, and Acrisius was killed by his grandson.

This made Perseus very unhappy, because he had not wanted to hurt his grandfather.

Perseus became king in his place, and he ruled for many years, a wise, kind and just ruler.

The Inheritance

The subcontinent of India, part of the great continent of Asia, has a long history. At least two of the most notable ancient civilisations lived and died beside its rivers. There is a feast of Indian legends, usually gentle and occasionally with an intriguing twist at the end.

        *   *   *   *   *   *

Once upon a time, a shepherd lived in a tiny village not far from Delhi in India. He had seventeen camels and three sons.

One evening as they were having dinner, the old man said, "My sons, I'm growing old, and I fear that I am about to die. You have looked after our camels well, and you need not fear poverty or hunger. But when I die, I'm afraid that you will become selfish and quarrel."

"Oh no," said the three sons. "We won't quarrel."

"I'm an old man and I know how people argue and fight. So I want you to know how to divide the inheritance I shall leave you when I die."

He turned to the eldest son and said, "You will have half of my herd of camels."

And to the second son he said, "You will have one third of my camels."

89

Then he spoke to the youngest son and said, "And you will have one ninth of the camels. Do not forget, that is my will."

The sons promised their father that they would do as he wished and they all went to bed.

In the morning, the three sons were sad to find that their father had died during the night. Then after the funeral, they tried to divide the inheritance as their father had wished, but they could not work it out.

The eldest said, "Father bequeathed me half the camels, but half of seventeen is eight and a half. How can I take half a camel?"

"You could of course take only eight and leave us to share the rest," said the other two brothers.

For a long time they quarrelled, then the youngest had an idea.

"Let's share the camels as best we can, and if one of us gets more than he should, he can give the one who gets less, one or two baby camels when they are born."

At this the two older brothers sprang up and began shouting.

"We'll do nothing of the sort," said the eldest. "What if the mother camel dies?"

"And what if the camels get a disease?" said the other brother.

The youngest son did not know what to say, so he shouted, "Then *you* make a better suggestion."

Just then a holy man was passing the house on his

old camel and he heard the commotion. He reined in his camel and asked, "Why are you quarrelling?"

The brothers stopped shouting and looked up at the old man. "We don't mean to quarrel. It's because we can't see how to divide the inheritance which our father left us," replied the eldest.

All three of them told the holy man how their father had left them seventeen camels, and now they could not divide them according to his wish.

"The solution is very simple," said the holy man. "I will help you. First take this camel of mine, then divide the herd peacefully and stop quarrelling."

"We couldn't do that!" exclaimed the brothers. "It wouldn't be fair to deprive you of your property."

"Don't worry, I shan't be any poorer!" replied the holy man.

So the brothers took his camel and added it to their own herd.

"Now let us divide the herd," said the holy man. "With my camel, there are eighteen camels, so the eldest of you who is to have half the herd will get nine camels."

He turned to the second son. "You are to get a third of the herd, and one third of eighteen is six. So you will get six camels."

And to the youngest son he said, "You are to receive a ninth. One ninth of eighteen is two, so you will have two camels."

The first brother took his nine camels to one side, the second led six away and the youngest took the reins of two more. Then to their surprise they saw that the holy man's camel was left over and was standing by itself.

Quietly the holy man climbed back on to the camel, smiled at the brothers and said, "You see, there is no need to quarrel if you stop to think for a while."

Then he went on his way.

The Tortoise and the Lizard

Over five hundred different kinds of people live in Africa, all with their own history and life style. Their names seem strange—but if you know the meaning, they are not quite so strange. Most people have heard of the Zulus—did you know it means "People of Heaven"?

African fables have an appealing simplicity and sometimes a stark ending, as in this one.

*　　*　　*　　*　　*　　*

One day the tortoise looked into his cupboard and found he had no salt left. So he went to see his brother to ask if he had any to spare. Luckily his brother had plenty, and said he could have as much as he could carry home.

Then his brother asked, "But how will you carry it?"

"That will be quite easy," replied the tortoise. "We can make up a parcel, tie it with string, and I can drag the parcel along the ground behind me."

"That's a splendid idea!" said his brother.

So together they made a neat package of the salt. Then the tortoise tied a long piece of string around it, took one end of the string over his shoulder, and set off for home.

He was getting along fine when suddenly the parcel became very heavy and he had to stop. When he turned round, there was a large lizard sitting on top of his parcel.

"Get off!" said the tortoise crossly. "How can I drag my parcel home if you are sitting on top of it?"

"It's *not* your parcel," replied the lizard. "It's mine. I found it as I was walking along the road, so now it belongs to me."

"What nonsense!" said the tortoise, getting very angry indeed. "It's mine."

They argued and argued for a long time, until at last the lizard said with a smirk, "There's only one way that we can decide whose parcel it is. We will have to take our case to court and let the elders decide."

94

The poor tortoise had to agree, and together they went to court.

The elders listened as the tortoise explained that he always dragged parcels along the ground behind him, because his arms and legs were so short he had no other way of carrying things. Then the lizard claimed that he had found the parcel beside the road, and therefore it was his.

The court discussed the matter for some time, but they could not decide who owned the parcel of salt. So eventually they decreed that the parcel should be cut into two, and each animal would get half.

The lizard thought that this was an excellent idea. Taking the parcel, he cut it into two, and carefully carried his half home.

Now the poor old tortoise had a dreadful problem, because the piece of cloth that had wrapped up the salt was not large enough any more. The salt spilled out as he dragged the parcel home. When at last he got there, he was very disappointed, for there was hardly any salt left. The long journey had tired him out, and he had to rest for a whole week.

While he was resting, the tortoise began to think up a plan to get even with the lizard. Although he was slow, he was extremely cunning, and a week later, his plan made, he plodded along the road to the lizard's home.

When he arrived, the lizard was sitting in his garden, basking in the sun. Slowly the tortoise crept up behind him, and put his great shell across the lizard's body.

"Look what I've found!" cried the tortoise.

"What do you mean?" asked the lizard, wriggling furiously to get away.

"Well," said the tortoise, "I was just walking along when I found something beside the path. So I'm sitting on it, and now it belongs to me—just like you found my salt the other day."

The lizard screamed and wriggled, but the tortoise would not let him go.

"You are mine," he said, "because I found you. There's only one way that we can decide who you really belong to. We must take our case to court, and let the elders decide."

The elders listened as the tortoise and the lizard

told their stories to the court. Then the oldest of them, a man with an extremely long white beard, said, "We had a case like this quite recently, about a package of salt. We must therefore, in all fairness, give the same judgment today as we did then."

The rest of the elders sat there, nodding their heads in agreement.

"We must cut the lizard in two, and the tortoise shall have half."

"A fair judgment!" said the tortoise. And seizing a knife, he sliced the lizard in half.

The Coomaka Tree

According to West Indian legend, the Caribs were the first men on earth, on the islands of the West Indies in the Caribbean Sea.

*　　*　　*　　*　　*　　*

In the beginning, long long ago, when only animals lived upon the Earth, the world was a dull and dismal place.

From their home on the moon, the Caribs noticed that the Earth never shone like the stars. As each year passed, the world seemed to grow greyer and dirtier.

"Let's go and clean up the Earth," the Caribs said to one another. So they set off from the moon in their

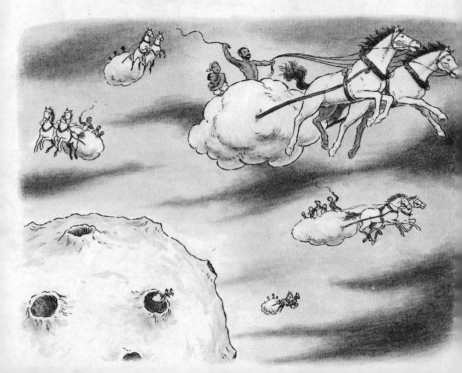

cloud chariots, and landed in the West Indies.

The youngest of them cleaned the plains until the grass glistened and the streams shone. The women polished the valleys and the small hills, until the flowers and trees sparkled in the sunlight. The men scrubbed and burnished the high ground and the mountain ranges, while the strongest of them drove away the clouds.

Then, when the Earth was clean and beautiful, the Caribs decided to return to their home on the moon. It was then that they discovered that their cloud chariots had broken loose and disappeared.

They prayed to Kabo Tano, their god who lived on a high mountain, but he did not hear them. The Caribs were now lost and alone on the Earth.

By now they had eaten all the food that they had brought from the moon. Far and wide the hungry Caribs wandered in search of food, but they could not find any. They all became thin and weak. Once again they cried out to Kabo Tano, and this time he heard them and answered their prayers.

In the forest he planted a huge Coomaka Tree, a strange tree that no one had ever seen before. Each branch bore a different kind of fruit. One branch hung heavily with oranges, another bowed low to the ground with great bunches of bananas. Yet another branch had mangoes growing on it, and from the roots grew potatoes, yams and maize.

A wild pig was the first to discover the tree, but he was selfish and kept the secret to himself. Soon the Caribs noticed that the wild pig which had been so very thin was now growing sleek and fat.

The Caribs knew he must have found some food. They tried to follow him, but he heard them as they walked through the long grass, and he hid in the bushes.

Since they could not trail the wild pig, the Caribs asked the woodpecker to follow him.

"We cannot follow him because he hears our footsteps. But he will not hear the woodpecker as he flies through the air," they said to one another.

Next day the woodpecker set out to follow the wild pig. Silently he flew through the air high above the trees. Unfortunately the woodpecker was a very stupid bird. Although he made no noise as he flew through the air, every so often he would stop and perch upon an old tree and peck at the trunk, as woodpeckers like to do. At first when the wild pig heard the tapping, he took no notice. Then, as he went further into the forest, he realised that the tapping sound was following him.

"Someone is trailing me," he said to himself. So that day he did not go to the Coomaka Tree which Kabo Tano had planted deep in the forest.

The Caribs were disappointed that the woodpecker had not been able to follow the wild pig, so they asked another animal to trail him. This time they asked the rat. They chose the rat because he moved quietly and

with such care. They thought that the wild pig would not notice that he was being trailed.

Next morning, the rat silently followed the wild pig. Every so often, the wild pig would stop and listen for the sound of the woodpecker. When he could hear no tapping, he made his way quickly to the Coomaka Tree.

The rat was just behind him, and when he saw the bright yellow bananas, the oranges and all the other fruit hanging from the tree, he decided that such treasure was much too good to share with the Caribs. There were so many of them that there could not possibly be enough for everybody.

That evening the rat returned to the Caribs and pretended that he had not been able to follow the wild pig.

The Caribs believed him, and asked him to try to follow the wild pig the next day. Day after day the rat went off early in the morning, and every night when he returned he would sadly shake his head and say that the pig had got away from him once again.

However, the Caribs noticed that the rat was getting fatter. No longer did his ribs show through his skin. One Carib, who had keener eyesight than all the rest, saw scraps of food sticking to the rat's whiskers when he came back one evening. Then the rat had to confess that he had found the giant Coomaka Tree. The following day the Caribs tied a rope round the rat's neck, and made him lead them to the tree.

At the sight of so much food, the people fell to their knees and sang a song of praise to Kabo Tano. Then to their astonishment, a voice rang out from the heavens saying, "Cut the tree down!"

The Caribs were amazed, but they had to obey the gods, and they set about felling the tree with their stone axes. The task took them almost a year, and at the end of ten months the great Coomaka Tree fell to the ground with a sound like thunder.

Then each man took many cuttings from the branches and the roots, so that to this day, every Carib has food growing close to his home.

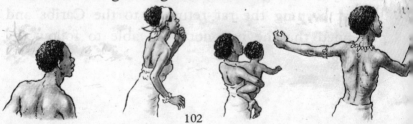

The She-Wolf of Indian Arm

When white people discovered North America, they found a native Indian people living there: we often call them Red Indians to distinguish them from the people who live in India. They lived peacefully in large tribes, but could be fierce warriors when it was needful. Much of their early history is lost in the mists of legend.

*   *   *   *   *   *

Long, long ago, before white people discovered America, the Indians lived in all parts of the land. Some lived in tepees on the great rolling plains, some lived in caves, and others in homes of mud-baked brick.

The people of Indian Arm lived in great homes made from cedar wood. The houses were so big that whole

tree trunks were used for posts and beams. Each enormous house had just one family living in it, with uncles and aunts, grandfathers, grandmothers and cousins all sharing. Relatives were very important people.

In one great house lived the chief and his family. The other great houses of the tribe were built close by, in a row above the beach upon which broke the waves of the rolling ocean. Behind the houses stretched the dense forest of tall cedar and pine trees.

From the forest and the sea came food. Some men were fishermen, others were hunters. Life was hard, for danger always lurked in the forest or the sea.

Not all the dangers could be seen. Disease and illness could strike without warning, and whole families and villages would die, for in those days the only medicines were the wild herbs from the forest.

Such a catastrophe struck Indian Arm, when a terrible sickness came to the village. It was so bad that fathers were too weak to hunt and fish for food, and mothers could not cook or tend their children. They sat listlessly in their chairs, or lay in their beds until gradually, one after the other, they died. At last the only one left was a tiny baby boy.

Hungry and cold, the baby lay in its wooden cradle with no one to look after it. Apart from the sound of the baby's crying, the village was silent. Then even the crying ceased, as the baby fell asleep.

On the edge of the forest, a she-wolf stood, puzzled. There were no men digging clams on the beach, and no children playing on the sand. No smoke rose from the blackened smoke holes on the roofs of the houses. All was quiet.

Softly the wolf crept forward, sniffing the air and listening. At last, satisfied that no harm threatened her, she became bold and padded about looking for food.

Outside there were only a few dry bones picked clean by the gulls. Then the she-wolf caught the smell of food from the house where the baby lay.

Cautiously, ready to flee at the first sign of danger, the wolf stopped by the carved doorpost and looked inside. She waited a moment, then slipped into the house and sniffed at the dried meat and fish hanging from the roof beams.

Beside the ashes of the fire, she found a half-cooked meal. She began to eat quickly, then suddenly the whimper of a baby made her prick up her ears.

For a moment she stood motionless, every hair and muscle taut, expecting danger. A soft movement in a wooden cradle attracted her curiosity, and without a sound she crept across the room. Then, licking her lips, she peered into the lonely baby's cradle.

The she-wolf gave a soft whine when she saw the baby curled up in the tiny cot. This was a man cub.

She gazed with steady yellow eyes at the tiny face all puckered up as the whimper turned into a frightened wail. The man cub reminded her of her own four cubs waiting for food in their den on the hillside.

But where was the mother? This baby was hungry and alone. For a moment she hesitated, and looked around the room again. Surely this small creature must be cared for? There seemed to be no one to look after this man cub. Then she made up her mind. She picked up the baby in her powerful jaws and started for home.

The child was heavy. Several times on her journey through the fir forest the wolf had to put him down and rest. She carried him gently, and it was hard to hold him.

The wolf cubs were whining with hunger when their mother arrived at the den. She lay down beside them and stretched out her body so that the little ones could get her milk. She knew that the man cub was hungry too, so she put out a paw and drew him close, and he was fed like the young wolf cubs.

Cuddling up to his warm hairy brothers and sisters, he soon forgot the cedar wood house, and felt that the den had always been his home.

The child grew up big and strong. He played tag and hide and seek with the cubs, and the she-wolf and her mate treated him as their own. They were very proud of the boy who walked on two legs and had no fur on his body.

Living with the wolves, he became a fine hunter, able to move through the forest without being seen or heard, and learning to run almost as fast as the deer.

When he became a young man, he started to go exploring by himself. One day he went far through the forest until at last he came to the seashore and the village where he had been born.

He stared in amazement at the great empty houses now falling into ruins. Who had lived there? Certainly not wolves.

Long grass grew all around each house, and there were even trees and bushes inside, growing through the roofs.

Inquisitively he explored the ruins, and examined the tools and wooden dishes he found.

What were these strange things? Hidden in one corner, sheltered from the rain and the weather, he found a bow and some arrows. For a while he played with them, then he fitted an arrow on to the string and sent it flashing through the air. He tried again and

again, and soon he could send an arrow flying straight and true at whatever he aimed. Excitedly he took the bow and arrows home to show the wolves, and the next day when hunting with his foster brothers he killed a deer with an arrow.

As the years passed and he grew older, he began to wonder if there were any others like himself. At last he decided that he must go away and search for them.

He said goodbye to the she-wolf and her family, and travelled far across the mountains to the rolling plains. Then one day he stopped at the top of a low hill, looking down upon a group of people who lived in curious pointed dens. They were the Indians of the plains, living in their tepees.

The plains Indians welcomed the young man. They offered him a home and promised to show him the ways of men. He learned quickly, and before long he married a pretty young girl from the tribe.

He told her of the beautiful country he had come from, with its great forests and mountains and the sea. It sounded wonderful to his bride, and she agreed to return there with him. After many weeks of travel they arrived at the ruined village where he had been born.

They settled down there to live, and had many children. Time passed, and the village was filled once more with busy happy people. The man became chief of the tribe, and on the doorpost of his house was carved the crest of the tribe—the head of a wolf.

The Wagtail and the Tribesmen

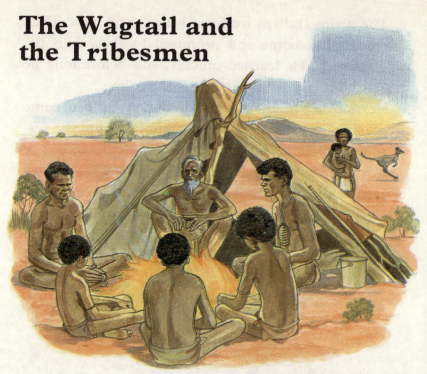

When Captain Cook visited Australia in the eighteenth century, he found a native Australian race already there—the Aborigines. They have probably been living there for the last ten thousand years, and they have a rich heritage of culture and legend, from which this story is taken. Their religion has as its core the "dream-time", where life continues always. It is the spirit home of a person, perhaps something similar to the Christian soul.

The wagtail of the story is a small bird, as common in Europe as in Australia.

Sitting in front of his tiny shelter beside the camp fire old Nanga looked out across the plain and watched a kangaroo in the distance.

It was evening and not the time for hunting, it was the time for stories.

So he began—"In the dreamtime, long long ago, there was no sea, only lakes and swamps. A wagtail lived in a fine well-watered land where there was plenty to eat—fruit, fish, roots and sweet honey.

"One day the wagtail went on a journey to the north and he did not come back for a long time. While he was away, tribesmen came down on to his land, even though they knew it was his. They built themselves shelters and lit fires, and grew fat and strong on the good food, the fruits, the fish, the roots and the sweet honey that belonged to the wagtail.

"Then one day the strangers looked to the north and they saw the wagtail returning. So they went and caught fish and cooked them, and offered them to the wagtail when he arrived back at his home. But wagtail was so angry with the men who had settled on his land without his permission that he would not touch the fish they had cooked for him.

"He did not even speak to them, but he took his spear and went over to the water-hole where they had caught the fish. Then he thrust the spear down into the middle of the water-hole and splashed the water round and round.

"As the wagtail splashed the water, it rose higher and higher until at last it covered all the land and drowned the men who had settled on his land.

"Then the carpet snake came out of the ground and made great hollows in the land, and the water flowed into the hollows and filled them. That is how the rivers and creeks were made.

"The rivers and creeks carried the rushing water to the edge of the land, and that is how the sea was made."

Slowing up the Sun

If you look at a map of the world, you will find the Polynesian islands scattered over the eastern Pacific Ocean. Although the people who live there are now Christian, they once believed in many gods. They thought of the sun and moon and other things in nature as beings with feelings and thoughts much as themselves, but with a supernatural power they called *mana*.

*　　*　　*　　*　　*　　*

"The days are much too short," said Mani's mother. "The sun goes so fast that although I prepare food and put it into the oven at first light, as soon as we see the sun, it's dark again before the food is cooked. And the nights are so long that no one can work."

"Then I shall have to slow down the sun for you," said Mani cheerfully.

"No one can do that," said his mother. "The sun is stronger than all the men of Hawaii put together."

"Don't worry, Mother! I shall use my brains and be very cunning." Mani started to think about it. "Now, how many legs has the sun got?"

"Sixteen," replied his mother. "That's why he can run so fast."

"If I could cut off his legs, that would slow him down," said Mani.

"Or perhaps you could catch him and then threaten him with a magic club, which is supposed to be the only way to make the sun do as he is told!" his mother said, laughing.

She thought for a while, and then said, "I'll make you some ropes to help you to catch the sun, then you must go to the crater on top of the mountain. There, each morning, the sun stops for his breakfast. Your grandmother cooks it for him, and she will be able to help you."

Mani's mother made the ropes for him from the leaves of coconut trees, and next evening he set out for the crater at the top of the mountain. It was still dark, but he could see his grandmother's fire as she prepared breakfast for the sun.

The old lady could not see too well. She had looked at the bright light of the sun so often that it had made her almost blind.

Softly Mani crept up behind her, and watched her preparing the sun's breakfast.

This morning she was going to roast some freshly gathered bananas for him. They lay behind her on the grass, ready to her hand.

Mani reached out silently and took away the great bunch of bananas. When his grandmother felt behind her for the fruit, she was puzzled.

"Strange," she muttered, running her hands over the grass.

Then she realised that they had been taken. She turned her head from side to side, sniffing the air. At last her nose told her where Mani was.

"Ah!" she cried. "I can smell you. Tell me who you are, or I'll kill you."

She picked up a huge club which glowed in the darkness, and held it over her head. Mani realised it was a magic club.

"Stop!" he cried. "I am Mani, your grandson."

The old woman lowered the club. "Come over here," she ordered, "and let me run my fingers over your face."

He stepped forward, and his grandmother put her hands on his face. "Yes, you are my grandson Mani," she said. "What are you doing here?"

He told her why he had come, and he asked her to

help. For a little while she sat thinking, then she said, "Yes, I will help you. I'm growing tired of feeding the sun every morning."

She gave Mani her magic club. "You will need this," she said.

Mani's fingers tingled as they took hold of the club.

"Now you must hide behind this rock and wait. When the first leg of the sun appears on the rim of the crater, you must catch it and tie it to a tree. When the next leg comes up, you must do the same thing again, and then again to each leg as it appears, until all sixteen legs are bound. Then the sun will be helpless. Use the club to beat him if he will not do as you ask."

From his hiding place, Mani saw the first leg of sunlight creep up the mountainside.

"That's the first leg," the old lady whispered. "Quick, catch it before it's too late."

Mani threw the first rope and caught the sun's leg. Then he tied it firmly to a tree. As one leg after another appeared in quick succession, he tied them each to a tree until at last there was only one leg left.

But he had no more ropes! His mother had made a mistake! She had made only fifteen ropes.

Mani grabbed the last leg and hung on to it, calling to his grandmother to bring him a rope. When she brought it, he was able to tie the last leg to a tree.

The sun could not get away. Slowly he dragged himself to the top of the mountain and glared at Mani.

"What have you done, stupid boy!" he roared. "Let me go at once." And he seemed to grow hotter and hotter.

The grass turned black and the trees were scorched, and Mani was burned in the fierce heat.

Mani turned quickly, picked up the magic club and brought it down on the sun's head.

The sun began to look unhappy. "What do you want?" he asked.

Mani told him of his mother's complaints. "You travel too fast," said the young man. "The days are far too short, and the nights are much too long. We have hardly got up before it's time for bed, and the nights are too long for sleeping."

The sun listened quietly while Mani spoke.

"If I let you go, will you promise to make the days longer and the nights shorter?" asked Mani.

"There's nothing else I can do," replied the sun. "Your ropes have weakened my legs, and your club has put a lump on my head. I promise."

And so to this day, the sun goes more slowly across the sky, and men and women have longer times to work and play. Only in the cold winter, in order to keep warm, does the sun go a little quicker, and then the days are shorter and the nights are a little longer.

Great Sundiata

Many, many years ago when there were great and powerful kings in Africa, the greatest of them all was Sundiata. He lived so long ago that now his story is mostly legend, but the legends have never been forgotten in the lands where he ruled. Mali was his country—a great land in the northwest of Africa—and his memory is still honoured there. Here is the story of this great king.

*　　*　　*　　*　　*　　*

Sundiata's father was a powerful king of Mali and a handsome man. He had a beautiful wife and two young children, a boy and a girl. In those days, the king was allowed to have more than one wife, and in time, he married again. The son of this second marriage was Sundiata.

When Sundiata was born, the wise men of the country foretold great things for him. He would grow up, they said, to be a wise and powerful king. He would rule over all the land of Mali, and his name would be known throughout Africa.

But as a baby, this great king-to-be was small and weak. Then when he grew older, he neither walked nor talked. His mother tried all she knew to help him, but it was no use. No matter how she tried, Sundiata could

not walk. He could only crawl.

The king's first wife mocked Sundiata and his mother. Her son Dankara was a strong and handsome lad, not a silent crippled child like Sundiata. She wanted Dankara to be king.

Though Sundiata was silent, he was no fool and his father the king understood this. He wanted Sundiata to be king after him, and he decided that his son should be taught the history of his land and his people. So the king appointed a special teacher called Balla for Sundiata. When Sundiata heard about this, he spoke for the very first time. "Come, Balla, and sit by me," he said, "and teach me all you know."

From Balla Sundiata learnt many things, for he had a

quick mind. But he still could not walk.

Sundiata was nine years old when the king died. He had wanted Sundiata to follow him as king, but the chiefs of the land would not accept the crippled boy. Instead they made his half-brother, Dankara, king.

Dankara's mother was so delighted at the success of her son that she made fun of Sundiata and his unhappy mother once again. Sundiata saw how his mother was mocked, and at once made up his mind to walk. He called his teacher, and told him to fetch an iron bar. When the bar was brought, Sundiata hauled himself to his feet, and from that day on, the young prince could walk. No longer were he and his mother mocked by anyone. Sundiata learnt how to fight and how to hunt. He made friends with princes from other lands. Then the people of Mali began to remember the great things the wise men had foretold for him.

Dankara's mother became jealous of this new Sundiata and began to plot to get rid of him. She asked the witches to use their evil spells on the young prince, but they refused. He had done them no harm, and so they refused to harm him.

This did not stop Dankara's mother, however. She hated Sundiata so much that she went on trying to have him killed. Sundiata was always in danger, and at last he and his mother decided that they must leave Mali.

At the age of eleven, the young prince left his native land with his mother and his sisters. His teacher,

Balla, had already gone. Dankara had sent him away to the court of an evil king called Soumaoro, and Balla was held prisoner there.

For the next four years, Sundiata and his family travelled from the court of one king to the court of the next. Sometimes they were welcomed as honoured friends, but in other courts they had enemies. The evil words of Dankara and his mother were spreading through the land.

When Sundiata was only twelve, one king invited him to play a game of dice with him. Sundiata agreed, and asked what the winner would have as reward.

"If I win," said the king, "and I certainly *shall* win, then I shall kill you."

"And if I win?" asked Sundiata.

"Then I shall give you anything you ask for. But I *always* win!" replied the king.

Sundiata knew that his enemies had turned the king against him. But what could he do? If he played dice with the king, the game would end in death. Yet he had to play, for he was the king's guest. So the game started, and the king played first.

As he rolled the dice, Sundiata began to sing a song. It was a song about being a guest in the palace of a king, and as he sang, Sundiata asked why a king should want to kill a guest. Could it be for gold?

The king jumped up angrily, forgetting the game. "Leave my land!" he ordered. "You must go, and your family too." So the little party moved on—then moved on yet again.

When Sundiata was fifteen, they came to the land of Mema, where the king welcomed them gladly. He took Sundiata with him when he went to hunt or to fight, and came to admire the strong, intelligent young man. The king had no sons of his own, and he wanted Sundiata to be his son and heir.

"No!" said Sundiata's mother. "My son is to be the king of Mali. That is what the wise men foretold, and that is what must happen."

During the years they were travelling, Sundiata and his family heard nothing of their own land. Were their friends alive and well? What had happened to

Sundiata's teacher, Balla? Was Dankara still king of Mali? Only after seven years was the silence broken.

One day when Sundiata's sister was shopping, she noticed a market stall she hadn't seen before. She went over to it, and found leaves and herbs that she hadn't seen since leaving Mali. She spoke to the people behind the stall, and discovered that they were from Mali.

"Come and visit us," she said. "Come today, for my mother and brother will want to hear your news of the land of Mali."

That same day the strangers came to see Sundiata and his family. His mother recognised them at once. They were no ordinary travellers, but important men and women who had known her husband the king. They had made a special journey to find Sundiata, the true heir to the throne of Mali.

The visitors' news of Mali was sad. No longer was it a rich and proud land. King Dankara had been defeated in battle. The country was ruled by the evil king Soumaoro (he who had taken Sundiata's teacher prisoner so many years before).

Sundiata listened to the news, becoming more and more angry. At last the visitors turned to the young prince and called on him to return to Mali.

"Your throne waits for you, Sundiata," they said. "Come! Mali is saved because we have found you."

"I will come," said Sundiata. "The time for words

is past."

He gathered together an army and set off for Mali. On his way, he stopped at those courts that had welcomed him during his seven years of wandering. Each king helped him by giving him more men for his army. The kings all hated and feared the evil Soumaoro, who had magic powers. All of them wished to see him defeated and driven from the land.

The strength of Soumaoro's army did not lie so much in the great number of his men but in the magic powers of the king himself. Those powers had always kept Soumaoro safe from harm, for swords and spears had no effect on him.

Soumaoro's magic powers frightened and angered Sundiata and his men. What could ordinary men do against such magic?

Sundiata called together the wisest men in the land, to see if they had any answer to Soumaoro's magic. But they had not. And if the wisest men in the land couldn't help, how could anyone else?

Then, just at the moment when Sundiata thought his cause must be lost, he found help. Two more people arrived—a man and a woman. The man was Balla, Sundiata's long-lost teacher. He had spent many years as Soumaoro's prisoner, and now he had escaped. He had brought with him Soumaoro's wife. She too had lived in the court of Mali before the evil king had taken her prisoner, then made her his wife. Though

she had pretended to support Soumaoro in everything, she had always been secretly working against him. She had managed to find out the one thing that could harm her wicked husband, and now she told Sundiata, "You need the spur of a white cock. That, and that alone, will harm Soumaoro."

When Sundiata went into battle against Soumaoro the next morning, he was armed with an arrow tipped with the spur of a white cock. He fought in the thick of the battle, but watching always for Soumaoro. At last he saw him, and the arrow tipped with the spur of a white cock sped from Sundiata's bow.

Though it only grazed the shoulder of the evil king, that was enough. Through that tiny wound, all Soumaoro's powers escaped. No longer could he laugh at swords and spears. No longer did he have magic powers to cheat death. Soumaoro fled from the battle, and his army fled with him. Sundiata had won!

And so the sayings of the wise men came true. The crippled child had become a great king. Mali became the greatest of all African kingdoms, and Sundiata's children reigned in peace and strength after him. The people of Mali will never forget Sundiata, the silent cripple who became the greatest king in Africa.